W0082725

THE INTERPRETATION
OF WAKING LIFE

Arkansas Poetry Award Series

THE INTERPRETATION
OF WAKING LIFE

Poems by Eric Nelson

THE UNIVERSITY OF ARKANSAS PRESS

FAYETTEVILLE   LONDON   1991

Copyright © 1991 by Eric Nelson
All rights reserved
Manufactured in the United States of America
95 94 93 92 91   5 4 3 2 1

This book was designed by Chiquita Babb in the typeface Bembo.

The paper used in this publication meets the minimum requirements
of the American National Standard for Permanence of Paper for
Printed Library Materials z39.48-1984. ∞

Library of Congress Cataloging-in-Publication Data

Nelson, Eric.
    The interpretation of waking life : poems / by Eric Nelson.
      p. cm.
    ISBN 1-55728-197-1. — ISBN 1-55728-198-X (pbk.)
    I. Title.
PS3564.E461515 1991
811'. 54—dc20   90-47289
                                  CIP

iv

ACKNOWLEDGMENTS

Thanks are due to the editors of the following periodicals in whose pages these poems first appeared: *Antietam Review:* "Kitchens"; *California Quarterly:* "Because the Air"; *Croton Review:* "Where Horses Once Were"; *Georgia Journal:* "Benediction"; *Green Mountains Review:* "The Spire"; *Laurel Review:* "Lovely until the End"; *Light Year 88/89:* "Everywhere Pregnant Women Appear"; *Mid-American Review:* "The Interpretation of Waking Life"; *Missouri Review:* "The Scene"; *New River Free Press:* "A Rock and a Soft Place"; *New Virginia Review:* "Here and Now"; *Panoply:* "The Calling," "The Door"; *Permafrost:* "Mrs. Mitchell's Needles"; *Poetry:* "Miscarriage," "Thanksgiving," "Pleasures of the Flesh"; *Poetry Northwest:* "Safe House"; *Shenandoah:* "Buttoned Down," "A Civil Tongue"; *South Florida Poetry Review:* "The Target" (as "KAL 007"),"Dance World"; *Sou'wester:* "An Old Woman on Simpler Times"; *St. Andrews Review:* "Team Effort"; *Three Rivers Poetry Journal:* "Natural Selection"; *West Branch:* "Deeper Channels," "The Measure"; *Western Humanities Review:* "Three Die in Seconds"; *Z Miscellaneous:* "The Trees of Knowledge"; *Zone 3:* "Horseplay," "The Snow Ghosts." "Because the Air" was reprinted in the 1986/87 edition of *The Anthology of Magazine Verse and Yearbook of American Poetry.*

CONTENTS

III

IV

For Stephanie, Benjamin, and Claire

I

BECAUSE THE AIR

Because the air hides nothing,
and dogs squat unashamed,
and squirrels argue in public,
and birds bathe in full view
of the cat who openly means them harm,
and spiders spin their deadly lace,
and flies kiss dung not caring who watches,
and fireflies flash aimlessly without regret,
and grass doesn't care if it's stepped on,
and trees don't take it personally
when they're stripped of their leaves,
or long for happiness or innocence,

he thinks that somewhere inside him
a life as quick and unafraid as these
must be hidden, buried beneath a city
of padlocks and façades.
And he thinks if he could dig deep enough
through the layers of fragments,
the arrowheads and bronze coins, the chips
of pottery, lead cups, wooden clubs,
clay tablets, hieroglyphs, and alphabets,
he would find at the source a heart,
his own, perfectly preserved and beating.
Brushing away the dirt and ruins of human
history, he would see it was the shape
of a leaf, a leaf clinging to a branch
with such inexplicable grace that he felt
moved to part his lips and utter *leaf,*
the sound of which made it fall.

NATURAL SELECTION

Magpies, Pliny tells us, are fond
of the human tongue.
They sit, heads cocked, listening
to talk far above their heads as though
it is a face they've seen somewhere.

One word, say "lips" or "yes" or "lava"
will stick, and they'll ponder it,
turning it over in their bird
brains like a mirror.
Satisfied by inscrutable logic,
they speak: yes, lips, lava.
Nodding, they preen and bury
their beaks in their hearts.

Sometimes they take a fancy
to a word they can't pronounce.
They brood, wrench their necks
grotesquely in their effort
to articulate a foreign thing—
"suitcase" for example.
They mull, gag, lose their appetites.
Weakening, they couldn't say it
if they could.

HORSEPLAY

1.

Stenciled indelibly
around swimming pools,
first words
from the lifeguard's mouth,
boldfaced bottom line
of the rules:

NO HORSEPLAY

An injunction so halting
it carried over
to schoolyard, parties,
ball games, trips in the car.

It conjured no image
but hovered malevolent
above childhood, waiting
to drag us, crying, to adults.

2.

Today I saw horseplay.
Ten or so grazed
in a gray morning—dew on the grass,
light fog, rain coming.

Suddenly one got uppity, kicked
back, shook head and tail, and bolted
wind-frisky for a small hill.
The others chased, mimicked the first
in a sort of horse's Simon Says,
mane wave and tail flip, a whirlpool
of buck and snort circling then breaking
to full-throttle sprint, slowing down
slowly, wheel and whinny, returning
finally their heads to the grass,
their sleek sides thumping.

THE GOOD SHERIFF

Just as we run out
of hope and firewood
spring suddenly shoots
green bullets through.

The wind, reformed,
confesses to maples.
The ground gives
up to tulips.

We rush out of our houses
laughing, clapping
each other's backs.
The children dance.

As the sun sets,
a shiny star pins
itself to the blue
shirt of evening.

We are so happy
we start telling lies.
We are so happy
we believe.

THE TREES OF KNOWLEDGE

He sits on his porch and stares
beyond the street of safe bets
to the park, pleasing green, shrubs
gangly with new shoots.
From thick sleeves of mulch
flowers flare up like parlor tricks.
The tall trees link limbs and drift
shade across the walkways.

Every electrical impulse that jabbed
him in his day dims now as the sun
cools and his mind assumes
the rhythm of the summer air.
His eyelids grow heavy as fruit.
No words turn in his head.

The hands that held each other
unclasp and hang like dead birds.
Gravity calls his shoulders, his chest.
An animal noise escapes him
and the brackish odor of fish
out of water wraps around him.
As his body hits the ground the wind
kicks up its heels and the trees
raise a rushing sound like applause.

THE SPIRE

We use it for direction. We're the house
beneath the tall dead fir.
Char-colored, lightning-split,
limbs tapered to needles,
no one is ever lost to that compass.

By day it is a jagged absence,
tent flap to night. At night
it is just darker than night.
Fall's flashy deaths cannot compete
with the fir's one sharp stab.
Winter can't white it peaceful.

Spring we make our beds and seed them.
We rest in the shade of the maple
and whistle through grass blades.
In the fir's ribs a cardinal
answers and vanishes.

A ROCK AND A SOFT PLACE

The sound wind makes on fluted leaves
could make me lie down in the traffic
of insects and let hawks eye my skin.

Drawing stones from a cold stream
to carry home, I choose one shaped
like a shoe, another like a one-eyed face.

Better a trap's rusted jaws, gnawed
leg, and lopsided escape than the human
heart chanting, I want, I want, I want.

In a cloud I see a violin, a gun, a bridge.
Bitter and small as words are,
I prefer a woman singing to a bird.

LOVELY UNTIL THE END

From somewhere my ear picks up
a piano note, knelled and echoing
delicate as a tea cup, not quite
emptied when another lifts
in the same light hand, some composer
alone turning to music a lake
he once took in and carried
until it turned to sound.

Radiant trees line the lake,
the day deepening by octaves,
crowded clouds edgy with rain.
In a patter of quarters, it sizzles
the surface as left hand claps thunder.
Top shags of the pines sway, brushed
by fingertips and scored to whispering.

It spirals down my ear, and I hold it
for the time it takes to pass
word for word, into sight.
Calm, the man on the shore sees
what he didn't expect, storm-churned
debris, bottom water, two fish
belly-up, bumping each other.

HERE AND NOW

1. The Applefalls

There's no urge like that drop.

Over the lawn mowers and construction,
over the swarm of insects gnawing
dry leaves of summer's parchment,

the rustle and thump
chills like a phone call too late.

Even in sleep, above
the swirl of fan and dream,

they knock all night.

Morning the apron of shade
beneath the tree is stained with apples.
And the tree bows with apples.

2. Listening

The first sound is not
the apple and not the tree
and not the air's shy advances.

The first sound comes from within.
We carry it around like a drop

of water, barely aware
until it falls, the only fear
we're born with.

We hear it as we see
a trace past the window,
the bird in the next yard already.

The first sound brings our eyes
up as the fibers holding stem to branch
crack. Then the broom-swish, leaf
rattle, and bunted limbs.
Then a gap, mid-air, before a voice-like
"don't" and the short roll
like a sigh, the bruise beginning.

3. Mid-air

Here when you dive in the pool
the drop of water in your ear disappears.

Here the body bathes itself
in its own acrid, sweet smell.
Here all the creases moisten,
the brackish taste of flesh echoes
along the tongue.

Here you've heard it all.
Here what you don't know would fill a book.
Here and now are synonymous.
Here the waitress will take your order
but forget to give it to the cook.
Here when you leave nobody notices.

Here a grave is just grass.
Here all dreams are the same:
just over the hill, another hill.
Here you live without patience.
Here nothing is about to happen.
Here everything goes without saying.

COLUMBUS OF THE ALPHABET

Where everything once was shriek
and pitch, throat-ruddered lurch,
or blubbering of the malcontent,

now mouth steers steadily
toward the spices and silks
of the new world, words.

Commander of his highchair, he
signals with outstretched arm
whatever wonders catch him

by shape or color, motion or sound—
pinwheel, clock face, backfire.
He claims all in the name of Knowing:

Buh: his mother, her breasts, me,
my beard, cat and dog, toys, food,
bib, light, telephone, everything

beyond the round world of himself
which he rolls to any edge and looks
to this other world, flat

as a syllable, where tree and sky
aren't separate but a single
brown, blue, and green thing: Buh:

a good word for a world so whole.
Yet even now his eyebrows, recently
realizęd, wrinkle downward.

A piece of paper like a sail
billows and dies in a fan's wind.
He opens his mouth but there's more

or less to this than he knows,
motion without motive, object without form.
He can't say where this wind has blown him.

II

THE MEASURE

At sundown the breeze lifts
leaves to their dark side.
The newly sprung flowers,
splashy upstarts, apples
of the sun's glib eye,
disappear in the dusky rubble.
The lawns, shrubs, houses,
all that stands still, fade
as the old edifice night
rises brick by brick.

In the dim resurrection
a single figure walks.
Only his movement makes him
visible, separates him
from the vegetable quiet.
The hushed birds, the
droop-lidded dog, the squirrels
prone in their limbs
watch him wide-eyed stride
through the night's wall,
the scissors of his legs
cutting the distance from then
to now to will.

Whoever he is, he is
earth's long ambition,
the ocean's secret wish.
Whatever he did today

he made history twitch
a little, like the muscle
of an eye, noticeable
only to itself. For him
the future waits, still.
Wherever he's going,
lone mover in the sky-
scraping pitch, all
the night eyes follow him,
prepared to wince.

THE CALLING

For years no one died.
Then, the marbled clouds churning,
all over town the telephones started
to ring like churchbells
yanked by a madman.

Every one was someone dead.
Strange voices trailed out
the holes of the receivers.
We stumbled from our houses,
cried our rain at the river's edge.
The sky broke over us in columns
like buildings, like the palaces
we dreamed we lived in.

Night fell, and the phones rang.
No one could raise a hand to answer.
Grieving we fell asleep, awoke
with the sun in our eyes
and ringing in our ears.

Absorbing Fire

Spring the mountains burned.
They looked the same, blue
low-rollers curving around the valley

unevenly as a hand-made bowl.
We woke and showered. Fed the kids,
ourselves. Fetched the paper

in a haze of green wood smoldering.
Still days smoke steeped the valley,
stained the siding. Breezy, between

blue bands gray currents drifted.
We worked, came home, watched
the news. The mountains became

weather. After highs and lows,
tomorrow's skies: mostly, or partly,
or only slightly smoky.

First Day of School

Evening air, still sluggish
with summer, lights clearer, cooler,
as it passes. On our skin,

at the roots of our hair
it pulls, harbinger of the far away
chill overtaking us, rippling

our own deep, cold wells in which
we drop our daily losses. Down the inner
ear they echo, monotone as whale song.

This weather like a lowered rope
raises them: days years
ago like this when we had everything

to lose. Yesterday. This morning
the six-year-old crying on the bus,
her mother crying as it pulled away.

Autumn's on Us

Shivering we turn to the house.
Busy ourselves with what
we can: weather-strip doors;

sweep the chimney; lay in wood;
check the furnace, the oil.
Replace all screens with glass.

Come winter snow
banking at the door,
wind storming the windows,

we're cozy to the fire, sipping
tea warmed on the radiator.
Fattened as the groundhogs

hibernating beneath the house,
we've long shut off what we know.
Any comfort turns cold.

THE WATER TOWER

Wherever I go I come back
to the water tower
by my house when I was old
enough to walk out
without saying anything
to anyone and ride
my bike farther than I knew,
into blocks like mine
but different somehow—
finer, brighter.

Then the day I'd been
riding toward arrived,
the day I went too far
and found where too far was.
Not just me but everyone
lost by turns, by stops
and starts, by choice.
My stomach tightened.
My leg shook on the pedal.
The distance between street
signs kept widening.

Suddenly the water tower
occurred, and I broke
for it, forcing
with each turn of the wheels

what I'd found
lost that day
and would find again
and again from my mind.

TEAM EFFORT

In Little League I learned the lesson
of the group—how many working together
are capable of more than one alone.
How the mediocre, like myself, might
shine in the team's larger light.

So when Woody Douglas pitched a perfect
game and hit the winning homer besides,
he told reporters it was a team thing.
The rest of us strutted the bleachers,
and I rubbed dirt into my knees.

My last year we made Regionals and played
on the greenest grass, smoothest clay
I'd ever dreamed. The fence was draped
in red, white, and blue banners. Two-tiered
stadium lights surrounded the field.

A real scoreboard with advertisements
towered behind center. Our first game
was a twi-night, and when darkness fell
completely, the lights became haloes
bathing the diamond lustrous as a star.

Late in the game, trotting to right field,
I noticed headlights moving slowly
through the broad darkness beyond the fence.
In position, I watched them over my shoulder
form a circle of double-barreled light.

The next inning that weird constellation
suddenly vanished, and a shock of orange
flame charged from the ground
to become a burning cross.
In the glow figures in white made a circle.

I turned and ran for the infield
between the first and second
basemen, past the pitcher, the coaches,
the umpire frozen on home plate, and dove
for the dark hole of the dugout.

Gradually the flame fell dimmer.
The cross shrank in roils of smoke
and finally disappeared. The circle
of headlights emerged again fitfully,
broke apart, and moved across the darkness.

Everybody on the field looked first
at each other, then back to the place
where it happened, empty now
as if nothing had ever been out there
but the swallowing night.

THE TARGET

How often the innocent stray
off course, betrayed by stars.
Cradled in the night's blue-black pitch,

half-moon winking in their windows,
they follow the drift of their dreams,
engines humming fatally over wrong waters.

What they don't know will kill them.
Mercy is not numbered
among the deeds of nations.

Sovereignty is sacred, and final.
Flesh and metal and tennis shoes
fall at predictable rates.

The last shred of human remains
drifts dreamless in neutral currents.
With every death-crested wave

breaking the shore, the bitter
widow knowledge mourns.
All she knows is grief.

THREE DIE IN SECONDS

I'm sorry for the dead,
but they're something else now.
No one can assume their posture,
the way their feet seem
jammed inside the wrong shoes,
arms screwed into stripped threads.

The illusion I can't follow
is a picture of three men
soon dead by explosion
standing quietly outside
an embassy in today's paper.
Short-sleeved, leaning, one stares
into his cupped hands
lighting a cigarette.
Another shades his eyes and strains
to see across the street.
The third stands like a man
impatient for a bus.

In the present tense of headlines,
they wait all over the world
never knowing what we do:
the cigarette doesn't get lit;
the blinding glare comes from behind;
luck is with the bus.

They have been something
else for hours now, bulldozed
rubble among rubble while the sun
set and moon rose, while the picture
developed and sped over borders,
while the paperboy stuffed inserts
beneath a streetlamp, while I wait
for the coffee, staring at them.

MISCARRIAGE

1.

Down of no comfort,
pillows for loss,
white feathers floated
over the hospital road.

One caught the windshield
and held a moment, small
flag of hope, then vanished
in the clearer logic of air.

On the long last grade
we overtook the flatbed
stacked with shivering geese.

2.

In the garden
the corn silk browned.
The ears spiraled
plump from the stalks.
Beneath the husks
a green worm worked
its way down,
gorging itself.
In its wake the offal
of its life hung.

3.

I drew stems of daisies
and zinnias from buckets
in the florist's shop,
pinched one in my numbed hand.
The woman smiled, said
they'd cheer a room and not
to worry, the hurt
stem would mend.

4.

The evening storm, first
only sensed, hit so hard
it was all there was
to see, to hear.

Gradually it slowed, disappeared.
Silhouettes of trees emerged.
Streetlamps glittered
on blacktop and rooftop.
We ate what we salvaged
of the corn, and it was sweet.

Deep in the night the air
flinched like a fitful sleeper,
and the rain stored in the trees
fell again.

MRS. MITCHELL'S NEEDLES

Dead nine months when we moved in,
she left reminders. Ghosts
of picture frames, stains
in the medicine chest, red polish
at 78 on the thermostat and at OFF
on the oven.

We got remover for the polish,
paint for the walls.
We shored the fractured steps,
replaced shutters, doorknobs, valves,
the full-length mirror.
We stripped, spackled, primed, finished.
We hung our prints.

The creaks and shifts that woke us
we don't hear anymore.
Still, where her shaking hands dropped
them, years of needles lie
snagged in the carpet.
With our shoes off
we step like guests.

THE SNOW GHOSTS

For rare snow I stopped
on the last bridge from home
to watch it and darkness fall,
beneath me a river of traffic,
windshield wipers dredging.

I knew in my shoes my socks bled;
the bridge iced before the road;
I had a warm place to go.
It wasn't as though the sky
was falling, though it was.

Across the bridge a snow ghost
swirled toward me, wailing.
I gripped the rail,
saw myself fall
into the river, idle
of engines the only ripple.

The red flash of ambulance
lights twirled in the distance,
speeding toward me or away,
I couldn't tell.
Coming or going, the siren
wailed like the dead
I never grieved for,
and the dead I never knew,
already gone and still coming.

A CIVIL TONGUE

To know leaf, my unnaming son
reaches for it from his perch
of father arms and bends
its stem like a bow, draws it
to his mouth and gums the light
green dark in his body's darkness.

Until his tongue becomes civilized
enough to hammer its roof,
patter back of teeth and retreat
like boys banging neighbor's doors,
lie still and let lips have
their say, he has no way

to take the outside in and claim
it, save taking it straight, swallowing
whole the whiteness of flowers.
How else will he know he can't get
sorrow from a turnip, laughter from a bone?
He must taste the roundness of ball,
the knife's truth, blanket's comfort.

He puckers at the ambition of books,
the longing of postcards, grins
in the permanence of dirt, the charm
of his mother's colored bracelet.
He frowns down the nothingness of mirrors.
From nothing outside, though, does he
absorb the ashy grit of death.
To that he must address himself.

III

THE MYSTERIOUS AND
UNEXPLAINABLE (VOLUME I)

My mother's firm belief
that there was nothing she could give her kids
more valuable than education

made her a sucker for grocery store
promotions of encyclopedias for children.
She wouldn't give the dish-a-week another

thought, but at sixty-nine cents for volume one
of any subject, she'd pick and choose
as thoughtfully as she chose vegetables.

At home milk sweated on the table,
hamburger bled in the sink, loaded bags
waited while we browsed the color illustrations.

My bookshelf swelled with volume ones, world after
*World Of: Insects, Animals, and Birds; Science
and Inventions; Great Explorers; Outer Space.*

Of all the vivid covers, I best remember
Continents and Nations, its African army
ants marching out of the jungle right at me,

and *The Mysterious and Unexplainable*—
the Abominable Snowman, blurred, shuffling
through blizzard over the crest of a mountain.

Eager for each new World, I didn't think
that full price for volumes two through ten
was more than we could afford,

that even learning had to hang
in the balance of food and rent, that
there was anything I couldn't know.

DEEPER CHANNELS

Far from water, this night wind
lapping spring leaves
carries me clearly to a fall
night on a boat in Baltimore Harbor.

We shivered
when the breeze came stroking
across the bay in sips, in ripples
as we drank our last drink together slowly.

Not knowing what we wanted
we searched by elimination,
starting with each other.
Denial is the first refuge of uncertainty.

Out there, in the dark water
beneath reflected lights of buildings
the blue crabs felt cold
moving in and dove for deeper channels.

We wondered where we'd be
in years and laughed when you said,
surrounded by our mistakes, then listened
to our laughter echo back.

Now I surround myself with mountains
far from water
and have come at last to love
the little good I am.

I don't long for that night
or any night I remember, though the wind
has a way of returning over water,
through trees, wonder.

WHERE HORSES ONCE WERE

Once upon a time this really happened.
Four friends went on a picnic.
They packed a basket of usual things,
climbed a nearly rotten fence,
and came to a stream lined with trees,
their roots uncovered by erosion.

They spread a blanket and ate
and watched a few clouds come and go.
They made a game of renaming one
as it changed: basket of flowers, ghost
ship, fish out of water, hornets' nest.
Drowsy with wine and summer they slept.

One woke and listened to birds
twitter about the stream.
He squinted at the orange sun and saw
shadows move over his friends.
Just as a fox disappeared he turned
and saw the tail as it flashed.

He woke the others who said
he dreamed it, and he wasn't sure.
Then two white horses with girls
standing in the stirrups cantered
where the fox had been. All of us
are dreaming the same dream, he answered.

THE SCENE

In the foreground, the four of us—my sisters,
Mother, and me—hamming for Dad's camera. Toothy
stage waves, a leg in the air, somebody's fingers
making horns behind my head as I grip the pistols
Dad gave me that morning.
                    Behind us, a crowd
of backs and backs of heads, shoulder straps
and camera bags. Lots of caps, short sleeves,
short skirts, and shorts.
                    Beyond them, across
the street on the sidewalk, a young couple
embrace in hard rain. In front and behind,
under umbrellas, in raincoats, people
on their way somewhere pass by.

●

Shooting our way through the French
Quarter, we saw the crowd gather.
                    Two men
hosed the sidewalk a long time before steam
stopped rising and glare disappeared.
                    The rain
came from sprinklers fastened to ladders, the
couple from separate trailers down the street.
The ones who walked past, the same ones over
and over in different clothes, amazed me most—
the way one person became another by adding
a hat, then another by changing a coat, hurrying

alone in one direction, slowly returning
as one of a pair or group.

·

That movie still runs, late. Two stars.
I watched it once but didn't see
the scene we saw filmed and filmed ourselves.
Cut, whatever happened in the rain
never happened.
                 I fell asleep before the end,
woke to snow on the screen. At first
I couldn't tell if what I'd seen
was movie or dream:
                 A man in bad clothes, dark
faced, floats out of nowhere into the path of a boy
and father. He flutters, hand out, mumbling.
The boy stares and steps toward his father who acts
as if the man isn't there. They pass right through
him into the street against the light. The boy
looks back. Nothing is there except empty
sidewalk winding toward a turn.
                 Though dreamlike,
long cut from memory's reel, I know I was there.
But where were my sisters, Mother?
Who was my father?

·

In real life, the actress drowned
after falling from a boat one night.
Others were there, somewhere else.
No one knows what happened.
　　　　　　　　　At reunions my father,
younger-looking than his age, his love my slow-
learned lesson, quietly presides. Family fleshed
out with husbands, wives, children, and grandchildren,
we slide-show our thirty-year-old vacation:
the four of us pointing to our hotel, posing
on Bourbon Street, standing in front of a crowd.
We don't believe our clothes and haircuts, how much
we've gained and changed. We point to the false
rain and couple in the background, explain
the tricks of a scene that appears nowhere
but behind us, in front of us.

LONG AGO NOW

Like pencil marks on doorframes, the linear shape
of childhood finally fades, outgrown or overgrown.
The way the lost loop back to where they've been,
the mind circles now and spirals toward the past.
As I read the story of missing Chester Cats
to my three-year-old I see my mother slumped
against the pantry, her face in her palms.
Almost as tall, I lean toward her, brace myself
on the counter where a few days ago I sliced
my index finger to the bone cutting sugar cane
and she held me, soaking the fear from my body.
I can't touch her, though I think I should
and want to, but not like that, absorbing.
I cross my arms, look down wishing I could go.
All she can do is cry, try to stop, and cry.
When she lifts her face I flinch at the red
blotches, puffiness, eyes I have never seen
pooled in tears, the whites all red.
She whispers it, barely gets it out before
she sinks away again: *Jollie Katz died this morning.*
Still I won't touch her, and I can't leave.
My voice, I'm suddenly aware, drones on outside
me: Sam Sunday has found Chester and brought him
home to the hugs of his brothers, sisters, mother.
I turn off the light and lie down with Ben, knowing
what he's going to say: *tell me a little boy story.*
It's part of the ritual, a story about when he was
a baby, a story he can't remember but wants to.
I've told so many now I've begun to make them up.

I tell him about the time he pulled a knife
from the table and put the sharp end in his mouth
before we knew, which never happened, but I know
the way his body tenses he sees himself take it.
He opens his eyes, *a big knife?*
Yes, big, I say, the one Mom uses to cut carrots,
and now I am beginning to see what never happened,
rushing to him and slowly pulling the knife
from his mouth, peering in for blood, scooping
him into my arms and holding her tightly, gently.

STRONG

for Claire

Already I miss you—your fingers
fishing my pocket for pen,
cigarettes, lint, whatever
you can grab and hold to sleep,

your head in the crook of my left arm,
crook of your knees on my right,
beside your crib in the darkness
you have always preferred.

Empty-handed, you curl it to fist
and raise it toward me, as if that
was what you wanted all along.
You are strong. Stronger

than your older brother
who has taught you nothing
is for keeps, no sooner
in your grasp than snatched away.

You accept it, the gift of loss,
and offer it—as you do toys
and food—to anyone who can take it.
You squirm to be laid down.

Ungently, I let you go. Yank
the side-bars into place.
By the time I'm at the door,
you're already breathing deeply.

AN OLD WOMAN ON SIMPLER TIMES

I don't remember when the milkman stopped
and Mother started going to the store,
but I remember Monday mornings, before light,
he carried two bottles and eggs and sometimes
a block of cheese to the door.
I imagined them two lanterns swaying
in the dark, up the sidewalk, onto the porch
where they shone like little moons.

When I came down my father was dressed
and pouring milk in circles over oatmeal.
My mother was at the window.
He kissed me, my cheek, called me daughter
of blue skies, a movie we'd seen.

Nothing changed when he stopped.
Mother started going to the store,
and sometimes I went with her. I liked
it there, bright and colorful and people
I'd never seen before smiling.
I never heard anyone say they were sad
the milkman was gone. Who ever saw him,
coming in the night that way?

I started high school that year and lost
my taste for milk, the film it left.
He brought it to me warm in a mug to help
me sleep. He pulled the bedclothes up
and kissed me, his robe falling open,

the mug growing cool on the night-stand.
When I came down the bowl was on the table,
and the smell of hair oil hung in the air.
It wasn't the end of the world, I hate to tell you.
Mother made her list and went to the store.
I'll tell you something else, it wasn't simple.

THE BEAUTY SCHOOL

In the mirror I watched her
face over mine judging
part and texture, splitting hairs.

Her hip firm to my arm
she lifted and trimmed,
blew wisps off the rim of my ear.

Pulling me close, she said
she'd never been this happy.
She always knew she had a gift.

She knew in a heartbeat
hair she'd cut, even if someone
else had done it since.

When she finished
she stepped away, slowly.
I saw myself in her eyes:

well-layered and shaped, all
she could do, but not
quite what she imagined.

THE AGE OF NECESSITY

Six moves by sixth grade, I'd decide ahead
what chips I'd chisel, what slivers swindle
from packing crates, relics archeologists
would envy: milk-glass hen's head, slick
veneer off a flat piano key, filigreed hinge
and knife tip I broke prying it loose, and
most prized, little finger of a figurine.

Each unpacking made my mother mourn and rage
against careless van lines—it's as if
they have to ruin them she'd say, sitting
broken on the loveseat with her checklist.
On my knees in my room, off-white and stale,
I'd arrange my pieces in careful rows
across the floor, admiring the shape they made.

DANCE WORLD

Blown trash lands here, a block
people say not to walk after dark.
Yet every night, between a take-out
and a parts store, Dance World's
picture window fills with
light and milling figures.

All pockets and good intentions,
the men line the walls.
Women cluster, going over steps.
Green feet taped to the floor
guide the uncertain.

The lesson of the night begins
with the couple who dreamed
and own this place.
In creased black pants and open
shirt, paisley ascot fluffed,
he calls the steps she follows,
auburn hair swept back
and lacquered down, pastel
dress tight across her bust.

Once through and again, silently,
smiling, quicker and quickening.
He glides as on ice, all grace and style,
her hem rises and twirls, lace
slip flashing as they slide, entwined,
the length of the room.

The students applaud, wonder, pair off.
Embraced by strangers, they start
with nervous laughter and talk.
Holding too tightly, they smell perfumes
rush the air, feel dampness
of palms bonding them.

Passing the window they take
their eyes from their feet,
see nothing beyond their own
picture—stutter steps turning
fluent, heels clicking lightly
together, arms curving gracefully
as wings.

THANKSGIVING

No charm rises from these chimneys,
no over-the-river-and-through-woods
greeting card air, no blue mountains'
comforting undulations, though there
are mountains, woods, and river.

Its sooty refuse bleeding down
cinderblock, smoke curtains
across mountains slashed open
for coal, side-gouged and banked
for space to park a house.

No one has business living here,
but mining is a business that pays.
Beside the tin shacks and trailers
a mound of coal rises lusterless,
a shovel piercing its side.

Dark as smoke, the river clogged
with garbage wrenches its way.
Trash hangs in trees where it rose.
Junked cars, tireless and rusted,
sink into soft alluvium.

Whatever thanks are made inside
these windowless homes, food
on the table, dry roof, dog
with three legs running
in its sleep, I swallow, hard.

EVERYWHERE
PREGNANT WOMEN APPEAR

Riding bicycles up hills,
lapping pools, volleying for serve.
There's one on any park bench, two
in any restaurant, three in any crowd.
In museums they gaze at the Rubens.
They're knee-deep along the beach
and up to here in advice.

Everywhere pregnant women appear
immaculate, shapely as pears.
Breasts like pears, buttocks
like pears, belly the biggest pear.
What they put in their grocery carts!
A whole cow t-boned, burgered, Delmonicoed.
Anything two-for-one, milk enough
to make Zion the land of just honey.

Everywhere pregnant women appear
like balloons rising over a fair.
Everyone watches their big tops billow
fuller than Barnum & Bailey's. Underneath,
the jugglers and tumblers, flying
trapeezers, lion tamers, clowns,
tight-rope walkers, and bare-back riders
limber up for their appearance.

BENEDICTION

Strapped in to your state-
of-the-art, space-age
infant seat, weighted
to the kitchen table, you look,
narrow eyed, suspicious,
as if you just landed.

Biology can't explain it.
I trust more likely sources:
strawberry field, stork drop,
clouds of glory, star stuff.

Little alien, welcome.
Now you cry to be here.
It's just the beginning.

Mystery of me, now you
raise your hand like a prophet,
reveal my heart's future.
It is poured out like water, it
is melted like wax.

IV

KITCHENS

Most open of rooms,
only here do you find
no mirrors.

The way some men
remember women,
I remember kitchens:
the smells and warmth,
the sweet hidden things,
the ghosts of mothers.

I may have been born
in one, like a kitten,
beneath the sink in the dark,
lemon oil over me.

Before the slow
spread of dawnlight, the flash
of kitchen windows.
Before the even flow,
the startling clang
of pipes, storm of water.

Any decisions that count
are made here, delicate
as dishes, final as knives.
Coffee steams a fine line
toward the smoke alarm.

On the refrigerator door,
messages and menus,
postcards and comics,
emergency numbers. Haphazard
pictures of ourselves
open and shut.

PLEASURES OF THE FLESH

He knows by his body
my fleshy body, deep-set eyes,
beard he yanks in handfuls.
My hands, having worked nothing
harder than a pencil,
are cushions to plump and cup,
ten paths to wander down.

Better than I he knows
my smell, my voice
soft as the feathers I brush
across his ears.
For my body his
body blooms every morning
as my face rises over his crib.

When he can name, say
father, the flesh made
word, words will fail.
As he fingers my cheeks, nose, lips,
he sighs so deeply
his whole body quivers.
And I, unable to express
myself, my body
long gone to my head, touch
his and whisper *face, face*.

THE DOOR

Not until I loved like this
did I dream this
kind of fear: as I make
the first cut into my son's
first birthday cake, white-iced,
edged with rosettes,
a cauldron of spiders pours out.

Calmed by water, I saddle sleep.
It strikes again as suddenly
as a stone rattles, uncoils,
flicks tongue and fangs.
Sleep bolts, venom enters,
flames a vision of him, gray
as ash in his crib, wrong-angled.

I want morning cries to wake me.
When they do I shuffle
muttering to his room.
When they don't I wait, staring
at the dark doorway, fear
so deep I feel it beneath years
and layers of fat ripple across
muscles the way it shudders along
the cat as it stares at a closed door.

Vigilant, finally satisfied,
it curls itself to sleep.
The door eases open, shadow angles in.

THE INTERPRETATION
OF WAKING LIFE

1.

Unlocked, the back door to dream opens.
A voice like footsteps whispers
There's someone in the house.
I turn toward sounder sleep,
but hands pull me back, Stephanie's
voice shaking: *Eric. Eric wake up listen
listen someone's in the house.*

I refuse and listen
for steps of the furnace lurching on or
joints still adjusting to winter.
By dream glow of night light I hear
nothing, but my breathing

suddenly seizes, catches
at a figure in our doorway fading
toward the baby's room.

2.

No dream yet everything
dreamlike, silent.
I rose and followed.
The hallway was wet, cold.
At Ben's door the figure
stood, motionless,
arms slightly raised.

For an instant it was
a photograph I studied for clues.
I saw a dim hall, at one end
a vaguely human form in a doorframe,
at the other a naked man frozen
in profile, ghostly,
open-mouthed. I couldn't stop
searching it or make it make sense
but I knew it was me

3.

shouting *Hey Hey Hey*
and everything snapped out of place.
The figure turned and
turned into a woman, hair glinting
with snow. Ben jerked awake and wailed.
The woman backed away from me saying *Beth?*
Where's Beth? as I stalked her and Stephanie's
voice behind me said *Ben, Ben* as she
pulled him sobbing from the crib and I pushed
my full weight hard against the woman, forced her
into a chair and stood holding her shoulders,
hissing *What are you doing?*
Why are you here? and I shook her and
I was shaking and I pulled her up, smelled
her drunkenness and dragged her
stumbling through the kitchen through the wide
open door and shoved her out into the darkness.

I bolted the door and went to Ben's room
where Stephanie, colorless, cradled him calm.
Between us in bed he fell asleep quickly.
We stared at the ceiling till dawn, silently
going through it again and again, fixing it,
erasing, imagining worse, wishing
we could go back and lock the door.

By daylight we moved warily,
guilt starting on us for the young
drunk girl who wandered lost into our house
expecting something and someone else,
who could have been beaten or raped or
frozen face down in our yard.
I opened the door and stepped back
from a drift of deep, unpredicted snow.

TOO NEAR TO COMFORT

Sleepless with worry I've forgotten,
I sat in the dark kitchen smoking, each drag
glowing closer to my hand, and I stared
at the window of my neighbor I barely know.

As if I willed it, his suddenly lit.
Wrapped in a dark robe he moved
from sink to table with a glass of water.
He sat, sipped, look out where he might

have thought he saw a shooting star flame out.
I'd slammed the cigarette so hard
into the ashtray embers stung my knuckles.
I watched him for some sign of seeing,

but he was looking down, chin to palm,
elbow to table, eyes hard on one spot
as if he were trying to burn a hole the way
kids do with a magnifying glass.

He seemed to slump from the weight of light,
and I wondered what had him up this hour.
Was it simple as dinner? A dream too true?
Did his wife know he'd slipped from her?

He buried his face in his hands, a gesture
so sorely human I wanted to turn away, turn
off his light and forget. Like a blind man
I felt my face, smelled smoke all over me.

HALF-LIVES

Get close to him
and quiet, you'll hear his artificial
valve tick-tick like that real fast.
Mayo clinic doctors put it in
just before he turned sixteen.
He'll be thirty-two this year.
This year he jokes
about his life and his half-life.

He's not to run, lift, strain, exert.
All of which I've seen him do,
and more than once
I've seen his hands grasp his chest,
his face drain, panic seize his eyes.
Twice he's been rushed
to emergency, once in a helicopter.
He can't afford the cost insurance
gives his odds, won't rent
a place that makes a lease, won't buy
anything on time.
             The last time
I could get up and go
with everything I owned in my car
was the year he got that scar he bears
like a cross from nipples to navel.
I moved from Norfolk to D.C. for no reason
other than it was the largest, closest
city and nothing was holding me down.
I met his sister at a party and found

how possessive I could be.
A year later we married. By then
he was in Baltimore in culinary school
specializing in pastry. He made our cake.

Since then we've bought and sold a house
and bought another, larger house.
We lost a child, had two more, filled
two floors and a garage. Everything's
covered: mortgage, cars, health,
old age, lives. When we die the kids will get
a little money and a lot of furniture.
We often wish for more and feel
some guilt for our excesses.
                              He's moved up
and down the coast—a summer here,
six months there—working pricey hotels
and restaurants until it stales
or a conflict with a manager or customer
erupts and he doesn't have to take it
He loads his truck and goes
somewhere else and everywhere
people indulge in fancy, expensive desserts.
He's no pie and cookie man. He's swans
shaped from pastry shell filled with mousse.
He's petit fours, napoleons, truffles,
sweets too rich for his blood.

He works alone before dawn, is gone
before the morning shift arrives.
He spends the day fishing or hunting
with his metal detector. Mostly he's after
Civil War relics, but he finds all kinds of things
people lose: wedding rings, keys, coins, watches.
He keeps it all in a locked chest
beneath the seat of his truck.

When he visits on his way
from one place to another, he stays
a few days roughhousing with the kids,
freewheeling some outrageous dessert,
keeping us up laughing, playing cards.
Usually I take a sick day, and we all
pile in the car and head for the shore.
When he leaves he leaves early, before
we're awake without saying goodbye.

MANEUVERS

Calmed by bedclothes, curled
to the shape spines
curve for, we wrap ourselves
in white flags, sleep a truce.
The pillows give softly in.

From far away a low roll
of thunder. Our eyes open
on nothing. Darkness squared.
Sound, literally, asleep.

Then again. Identical twin.
Deep echo tunneling toward,
like a road arumble with trucks
heavy with weapons.

Close, they brake. Idle. Throttle
and roll away from us inching
closer to clasp and whisper
before they come back ticking
gravel, surrounding.
We stiffen and wait for light
to strike the windows.

Choked down, the engines fade.
Rain's boot click and hurried steps
fill the street, fill us
as we sink into dreams we twist
tortured in, remember clearly
but do not confess.

SQUARE

Once the heavy stuff has been dragged out,
wept and argued over, muffled
in pads, the rest divides,
boxes up neatly.

Simmer of years—garlic, burnt rubber,
musk of dead mice in the walls, wood
rot and putty, stove crust—
evaporates like milk.

Windows, smoke-blurred, fingerprinted,
come clean. Dust is annulled.

The bared walls stand plumb.

Jut angle corner jag.
The hard edge below everything
rises from the shadows, shining.

RELOCATING

Unsettled as an argument, clumsy
as boxes, we moved away
from each other, went to opposite ends
of the house and lay alone, tossing.
Even the air was inverted, stickier
than we imagined.

The fan's steady wheeling, the shade
blinds made of light, that balance
of movement and stillness calmed
me to sleep, rapid with bad dreams.

Clouds darkened and dropped.
Air became wind.
Limbs rose and fell like wings.
Rain began.

When I opened my eyes you were moving
toward me, nimbused in storm light,
barefoot, your sleep-wrinkled dress off
one shoulder. Lightning
gutted the sky. All outdoors bent over

wildly as you bent soundlessly and lay
your head on my chest, held
my face in your palms. Urged

by flash and thunder, we tore
through layers, bit, shook less humanly
than the flailed trees resisting
every surge of minus and plus. Collapsed,

each labored breath
an evening, a familiar strain of neither
here nor there, we looked out the window

numb to devastation: trees snapped
in half, trunks split down the center,
limbs twisted as broken arms.
And one tree wholly uprooted,
the roots like a wagon wheel
mired in its own rut.

DAY TONIGHT

for Stephanie

Blanket-pink sky in the window, it is
evening, day slowed down, dinner heavy
in our bellies. We stretch out

on the couch, legs over legs, whispering
because the color of the sky says to.
Entwined, blood slowed, your light

slender legs and mine, darker, heavier,
lose feeling, become us apart from us.
Wrapped in you, I could wrap myself

to this moment, settle in your body,
sleep the sleep of the well-satisfied.
Already though, behind my back

pink's gone to blue, powder to smoke
so soon I barely see you.
Not yet night, night twitches nerves

along the backs of my hands. Blacks
of my eyes expand, black holes pulling in.
Now the tingle, the pinpricks, the needles

so sharp we have to pull ourselves apart,
hold our legs straight, tractioned.
At the window I see blue double-crossed

pink all along. Legs steadier,
I stare harder. What I am looking
for I find, turning in your eyes.

BUTTONED DOWN

Hundreds of miles, a time
zone from my life—yard burdened
with toys, cat at the door, family
wagon, a woman who could live without
poems but not a bed of herbs,
who wages war on weeds,
love on children—I hardly know
what to think of myself
so suddenly light.

I am as if I were
someone I once knew well and recall
tenderly. The way he never
buttoned his cuffs, how they slid
and flapped like white birds
dipping and feeding at his hands.
How he carried no wallet and kept
money wadded in his pocket like trash.
He led his life like a father
leads a child through a dark room,
saying in his steps, *here, it's nothing.*

Yet how afraid he was of what
became him—accumulation of quick
decisions, shifts in direction
that became a direction,
a bird veering from the flock
only to meet it
later on stranger ground.

Seeing him, I'm pulled again
to that light-footed stride, aloof
shadow skimming the surface.
I watch him rise. Wistfully,
without envy, I wave.

SAFE HOUSE

No more to us than noise, root and rut,
whispering tussle and occasional
clang of cans, we made every barricade—
mesh and brick, sandbag and two-by-four—
to keep possum out from under us.
Wherever we dug they dug deeper.

In a place we feared they might
enter the house, we pushed an old pink
bedspread they pulled through one night,
and we imagined them snout to belly, tail
to eye, pink spread plumped under them,
snoozing through our days: the storms

of flush and drain, clack of stacked
cans, the baby's thumps and howls,
stereo and telephone, our voices rising
and falling, long vowels and short
drifting like odors into another shape—
simple, dark, and hungry.

One morning through the bedroom blind
I saw one, still as a boulder outside
the crawlspace hole, eyes fixed inward,
dying of something I couldn't see.
All morning it dragged itself away, away
from all that was sound within.

Drifting to sleep that night we heard
them fumble awake, bump clumsy as ghosts,
scuttle out and savage our garbage.